For Nadine

This edition published in 1998

Published by Blitz Editions, an imprint of Bookmart Limited
Registered Number 2372865
Trading as Bookmart Limited
Desford Road, Enderby, Leicester, LE9 5AD

Copyright © Text Ernest Henry 1997
Copyright © Illustrations Joanna Walsh 1997
Designed by Lisa Coombes
The moral right of the author and illustrator has been asserted

ISBN 1 85605 407 1

Printed in Hong Kong by C&C Offset Co., Ltd
10 9 8 7 6 5 4 3 2 1

Rub-a-Dub-Dub

New and best
loved poems for babies

Ernest Henry • Pictures by Joanna Walsh

BLITZ EDITIONS

Contents

1
Hello, I'm Your Baby!

2
That's Not a Phone

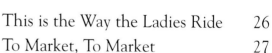
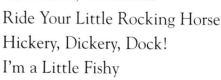

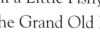

3
Let's Go!

4
Lulla Bye

This space is for your baby's first photograph,
or anything special that reminds you of those first months together!

1

Hello, I'm Your Baby!

Baby's here

And we're so happy
To feed him milk
And change his nappy.

How Many Days?

How many days has my baby to play?

Saturday,

Sunday,

Monday

Tuesday,

Wednesday,

Thursday,

Friday

Saturday,

Sunday,

Monday...

Action – count your fingers or toes, or lift baby's arms up for one day, down for the next.

I'm a Bunny

I'm a Bunny
You're a Bunny
Bunny, bunny, bunny, bunny.

I'm funny
You're funny
Funny, funny, funny, bunny.

*Action – hold
baby's hands
and jump around
– like a bunny!*

Upsidaisy

Upsidaisy diddledidumdo
Downsidaisy diddlededoo.
Upsidaisy diddledidumdo
Diddledididdledidum with you!

Action – up with baby's arms…
down with baby's arms…

Flying Baby

Flying baby:
Round and around
High in the sky
So far from the ground.
Uuuuuuuuuuup like an aeroplane
Swoooooooop like a bird;
Whooooossssshhhhhhhh like a rocket
Sssssshhhhhhhhhhhhhhh – not a word.
Then terribly quickly
All the way down –
And UP – flying baby
Round and around.

Action – hold baby firmly and
follow the poem!

Humpty Dumpty

Humpty Dumpty sat on a wall,
Humpty Dumpty had a great fall:
All the King's horses
And all the King's men
Couldn't put Humpty together again.

Action – sit baby on the knee.

13

The Cat and the Fiddle

Hey diddle, diddle
The Cat and the Fiddle
The cow jumped over the Moon.
The little Dog laughed to see such sport
And the Dish ran away with the Spoon.

Little Face

Little nose!

Little cheeks!

Little chin!

Action – gently point and touch.

Little Bo-Peep

Little Bo-Peep
Has lost her sheep
And doesn't know where to find them.
Leave them alone,
And they'll come home
Bringing their tails behind them.

Baa, Baa Black Sheep

Baa, Baa, Black Sheep
Have you any wool?
Yes sir, yes sir,
Three bags full.
One for my master,
One for my dame,
And none for the little boy
Who lives down the lane.

Peep Boo!!

Here's the baby's trumpet
Toot, toot-toot! Toot-too!
Now, where has that baby gone?
There he is – Peep Boo!

Here's a big umbrella,
Keep the baby dry!
Here's the baby's little cot:
Rock-a-baby-bye!

All For Baby

Here's a ball for baby,
Big and soft and round.
Here's a baby's hammer –
What a bashy sound!

Here's baby's music
A song that we all know.
Here are baby's cuddly toys
Standing in a row!

Round and Round the Garden

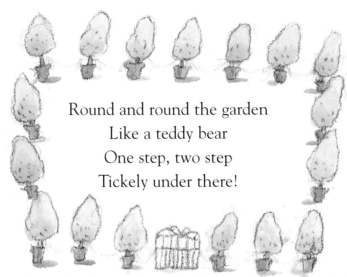

Round and round the garden
Like a teddy bear
One step, two step
Tickely under there!

Action – round and round with your finger on baby's palm, then tickely under there!

The Little Nut Tree

I had a little nut tree
Nothing would it bear
But a silver nutmeg
And a gold pear.

The King of Spain's daughter
Came to visit me
And all for the sake
Of my little nut tree.

You're All There!

Where are your little eyes?

Where's your little nose?

Where did you put your chinny-chin,

And where are those wriggly toes?

Show me all your fingers

– Where's that lovely hair?

Now turn around

And let me see that

You're
  – All
    – There.

Action – just follow the poem.

21

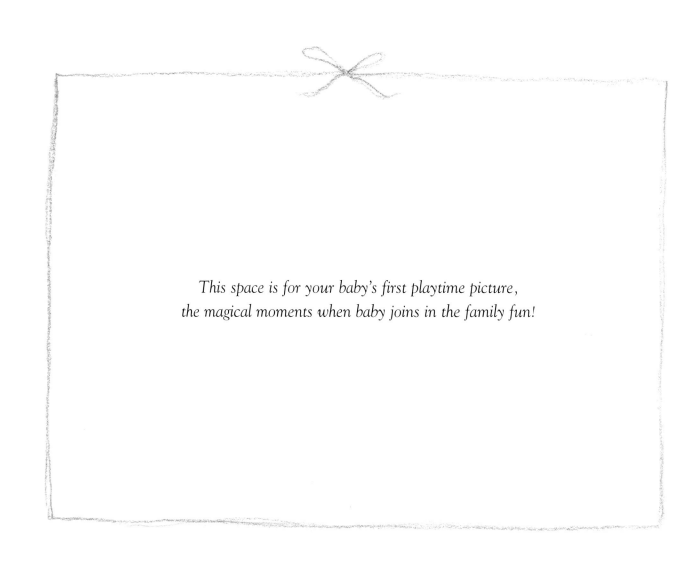

This space is for your baby's first playtime picture,
the magical moments when baby joins in the family fun!

2

That's Not a Phone… It's a…

That's Not a Phone, It's a Foot!

One,

Two,

Three –

One,

Two,

Three,

Four.

That's not a phone:
It's a foot!

*Action – take baby's foot in your hand, pretend to
tap out a seven digit phone number on the sole…*

Jack Be Nimble

Jack be nimble, Jack be quick,
Jack jump over the candle stick!

Jumping Joan

Here I am, little jumping Joan,
When nobody's with me, I'm all alone.

Action – jump about like a silly sock!

This is the Way the Ladies Ride

This is the way the ladies ride;
Tri, tri, tri, tri,
This is the way the ladies ride;
Tri-tri, tri-tri, tri!

This is the way the gentlemen ride;
Gallop-a-trot, gallop-a-trot,
This is the way the gentlemen ride;
Gallop-a-gallop-a-trot!

This is the way the farmers ride;
Hobbledy-hoy, hobbledy-hoy,
This is the way the farmers ride;
Hobbledy-hobbledy-hoy!

To Market, to Market

To market, to market,
    to buy a fine pig,
Home again, home again,
    Jiggetty-jig!

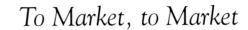

To market, to market,
    To buy a fine hog,
Home again, home again,
    Joggetty-jog!

*Action – bouncing baby on the knee
(careful with the tiny ones!)*

Ride Your Little Rocking Horse

Ride your little rocking horse
All over town.
Ride it up the high street,
Ride it back down.
Out of the supermarket,
Into a shop.
Ride your little rocking horse
And
      never,
          ever
            stop.

*Action – bouncing baby on the
knee if no rocking horses are available.*

Hickery, Dickery, Dock!

Hickery, dickery, dock!
The mouse ran up the clock.
The clock struck one:
Boiiinnnggg!!!!!!
The mouse ran d
o
w
n
Hickery, dickery, dock.

*Action – sit baby on knee, meet
heads-gently – at Boing!*

I'm a Little Fishy

In a high voice
I'm a little fishy,
I'm a little fishy,
Swim, swim, swim,
Swim, swim, swim.

I'm a little fishy,
I'm a little fishy,
Swim, swim, swim, swim, swim.

In a sweet female-like voice
I'm a lily leaf,
I'm a lily leaf,
Swim, swim, swim,
Swim, swim, swim.

I'm a lily leaf,
I'm a lily leaf,
Swim, swim, swim, swim, swim.

In a deep cockney croak
I'm a little frog,
I'm a little frog,
Swim, swim, swim,
Swim, swim, swim.

I'm a little frog,
I'm a little frog,
Swim, swim, swim, swim, swim.

In a thick accent
I'm a riggely verm,
I'm a riggely verm,
Swim, swim, swim,
Swim, swim, swim.

I'm a riggely verm,
I'm a riggely verm,
Swim, swim, swim, swim, swim.

In a sweet voice
I'm a butterfly,
I'm a butterfly,
Swim, swim, swim,
Swim, swim, swim.

I'm a butterfly,
I'm a butterfly,
Swim, swim, swim, swim, swim.

In a Spanish accent
I'm a naughty gnat,
I'm a naughty gnat,
Swim, swim, swim,
Swim, swim, swim.

I'm a naughty gnat,
I'm a naughty gnat,
Swim, swim, swim, swim, swim.

Refrain
I'm a little fishy,
I'm a little fishy,
Swim, swim, swim,
Swim, swim, swim.

I'm a little fishy,
I'm a little fishy,
Swim, swim, swim, swim, swim.

Action – washing and playing in the bath.

31

The Grand Old Duke of York

Oh
The
Gggggrrrrrand Old Duke of York
He had ten thousand men:

He marched them up to the top of the hill,
And he marched them down again.

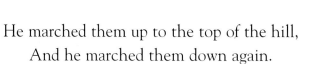

And when they were up, they were up.
And when they were down, they were down.

And when they were neither halfway up,
They were neither up nor down.

Action – bouncing baby on the knee.

33

Doctor Foster

Doctor Foster
Went to Gloucester
In a shower of rain

The Incy Wincy Spider

The incy wincy spider
Climbed up the water spout.
Down came the rain
And washed the spider out.
Out came the sun,
And dried up all the rain:
And the incy wincy spider
Climbed up the spout again!

Ladybird, Ladybird

Ladybird, Ladybird
Fly away home:
Your house is on fire,
Your children will burn.
All but one,
Her name is Anne,
And she crept under the frying pan.

He stepped in a puddle
Right up to his middle
And never went
there again.

Walking Down the Lane

One day,
little *_____ was wandering down the lane on
the way to the corner shop.
The sun was shining,
the birds were singing,
the flowers were all blooming and happy and
everything was lovely.

* Insert child's name

'What a lovely day,' said little *_____.
'Everything is soooooooo lovely!!!'

The sun is shining,
the birds are singing,
the flowers are blooming,
the sky is blue,
diddledi bom
and...

*_____ fell straight into a hole in the road.

*Action – up with the arms,
down with the arms, and
tumble between the knees.*

37

Little Piggie

This little piggie stayed at home.

This little piggie went to market.

This little piggie had roast beef –

To Catch a Fish Alive

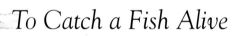

One two three four five.
Once I caught a fish alive.

Six seven eight nine ten.
Then I let him go again.

This little piggie
had none.

And this little piggie
went weeeeeeeeeeeeee all
the way home.

Action – counting toes

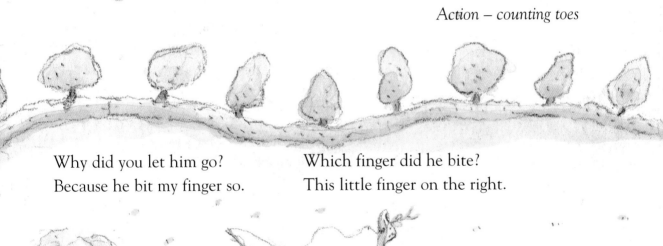

Why did you let him go?
Because he bit my finger so.

Which finger did he bite?
This little finger on the right.

Action – counting fingers.

The Story of Joey, the Finger

Joey the finger was a very sad finger, because nothing he ever tickled laughed.

He tickled the pillow – and that didn't laugh.

He tickled the table top – and that didn't laugh.

He tickled the lampshade – and that didn't laugh either.

Joey was very, very sad.

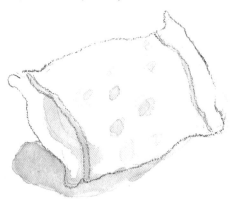

One day, Joey, the sad finger met Rupert's finger.

'Hello Joey,' said Rupert's finger, happily. 'Why are you looking so sad?'

'Because nothing I tickle ever laughs,' replied Joey.

'I tickle the pillow – and that doesn't laugh.'

'I tickle the table top – and that doesn't laugh.'

'I tickle the lampshade – and that doesn't laugh, either. Nothing I tickle ever laughs,' said Joey.

'I bet if you tickled Rupert, he'd laugh,' said Rupert's finger.

'Do you think so?' said Joey.

'Yes I do!' So Joey did.

And Rupert laughed; and Joey, the sad finger, was happy again.

Action – just follow the story!

Little Jack Horner

Little Jack Horner
Sat in a corner
Eating his Christmas Pie.

He put in his thumb
And pulled out a plumb
And said what a good boy am I!

Pat-a-Cake

Pat-a-cake,
Pat-a-cake,
Baker's man,
Bake me a cake as
Fast as you can.
Pat it
And prick it,
And mark it with B:
Put it in the oven
For Baby and me.

Action – hand clapping.

43

This space is for your baby's first action picture,
or something special to remind you of baby on the move!

3

Let's Go!

One, Two, Buckle My Shoe

One, two,
Buckle my shoe,

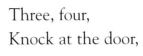

Three, four,
Knock at the door,

Action – counting.

Get Up and Going!!

Jumping and turning and
Thinking and learning and
Standing and stretching and
Carrying and fetching and
Laughing and shouting and
    In-ing and out-ing and
      To-ing and fro-ing and
        Get up and going!

Nineteen, twenty,
My plate's empty!

Seventeen, eighteen,
Maids in waiting,

Fifteen, sixteen,
Maids in the kitchen,

Five, six,
Pick up sticks,

Seven, eight,
Lay them straight,

And...

Hiding and seeking and
Peek-a-boo peeking and
Snoozling and sleeping and
Crawling and creeping and
Jiggling and giggling and
Wiggling and wriggling and
Growing and growing and
Get up and going!

*Action – bouncing baby on knee,
faster and faster.*

Nine, ten,
A big fat hen,

Eleven, twelve,
Dig and delve,

Thirteen, fourteen,
Maids a-courting,

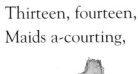

More Car

More car,
More car,
More car
Oh I love my little car.
It takes me very near
Or it drives me very far.

It takes me off to work
Or it takes me out to play.
We poddle in the park
And I use it every day.

More car,
More car,
More car
Oh I love my little car.

Action – say this one in the car!

Peep Peep – Choo Choo!!

Chug-a-ling-a-long-a-loo!
Hold very tight now – off we choo.
Can't be late so too-dle-loo,
We're a train: Peep Peep – Choo Choo!!

Chug-a-ling-a-long-a-loo!
We've got an engine bright and new.
You can come if you want to,
We're a train: Peep Peep – Choo Choo!!

Peep Peep – Choo Choo!!
Peep Peep – Choo Choo!!

Action – hanging onto Dad's trouser shuffling along.

Mr Sossy Man

Where is that Sossy man,
I haven't seen him here before?
Under the table,
Round the plate,
Through the window,
Out of the door.

Where is that Sossy Man,
Have you seen him buzzing around?
Up on the ceiling,
Under a mat,
There! In the corner –
What was that sound?

Where is that Sossy Man?

Action – feeding baby,
but follow the poem
and see what happens!

Polly Put the Kettle On

Polly put the kettle on,
Polly put the kettle on,
Polly put the kettle on,
We'll all have tea!

Sukey take it off again,
Sukey take it off again,
Sukey take it off again,
They're all gone away!

*Action – pretend to make tea
and baby be the teapot!*

51

Climb Up Me

Put –
One foot on my left knee,
One foot on my right.

Now –
Walk up my tummy...
...And give me a fright:

Boo!!

Ever So Small

Lie down on the ground,

Curl up like a ball,

Ever so tightly,

Ever so small!

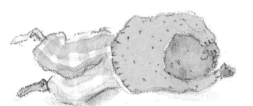

Pretend your invisible,
Don't make a sound...

Then –

Jump up

Like a rabbit,

Four feet off the ground!

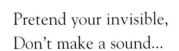

*Here is a space for a final photograph or drawing of the only time
in a baby's day when all is quiet... sleeptime!*

4

LullaBye

Up the Wooden Hill

Up the wooden hill to blanket fair
What shall we find when we get there?
A bucket full of water and a penny worth of hay

Gee up, Dobbin all the way!

Rub-a-Dub-Dub

Rub-a-dub-dub,
Three men in a tub:
They all had a jolly good scrub.

They scrubbed and scrubbed
And rubbed and rubbed
And then they went home for tea!

Action – washing in the bath, of course!

Hush-a-Bye Baby

Hushhhhh-a-bye Baby, on the tree top
When the wind blows, the cradle will rock.
When the bough breaks, the cradle will fall
Down tumbles cradle, Baby and all.

LooLa, LooLa, Bye, Bye

LooLa, LooLa,
LooLa, LooLa, bye, bye –
Do you want the moon to play with
Or the stars to run away with?
They'll come if you don't cry...
LooLa, LooLa,
LooLa, LooLa, bye, bye –
In your mother's arms a-weeping.
But soon you'll be a-sleeping, LooLa,
LooLa, LooLa,
LooLa, LooLa bye.

Little Head

Little head, little head,
Sweetly on your pillow,
Rocking gently to and fro
Like a swaying willow.

Little head, little head,
Full of fun and laughter.
Keep on. Sleep on, little head
And I'll look ever after.

Until Tomorrow Morning

Now it's the end of another day,
We've worked our work
and we've played our play,
It's time to sleep and dream away
Until tomorrow morning.

We've done so much and travelled so far
From here to the shops and to Zanzibar.
We've tied up the ship and parked the car
Until tomorrow morning.

The moon has come to chase the sun,
See it smile down on everyone.
The stars will twinkle in play and have fun
Until tomorrow morning.